Contents

About This Book

This book provides engaging ideas to help
children develop skills in creative writing
and in constructing nonfiction texts.
Children need to learn the language,
structure, and conventions of different kinds of
writing before they can start writing confidently on their own.
They need to repeatedly hear and read stories they can then
talk about, retell, and draw upon to invent their own.

The Value of Fairy Tales

The four well-known fairy tales in this book will stimulate
children's imagination and creativity. These stories all have simple,
straightforward plots and clearly identifiable good and bad characters.

The settings, such as castles in the sky or houses peopled
by bears and pigs, are fantastically make-believe.
Scary or magical events—a talking wolf who can climb down
a chimney; a fairy godmother who can transform a pumpkin
into a coach, and a beanstalk that grows
up into the clouds—evoke wonder and suspense.
In the end, bad characters such as the big, bad
wolf, the giant, and the stepsisters,
are punished and the good characters
live happily ever after.

Such inventive tales are full of possibilities for adaptation
and many of the writing activities in the book encourage this.
They can also be used as starting points for children
to write their own stories.

How the Book Works

This book is divided into four chapters. Each one opens with an illustrated retelling of a fairy tale, ideal for sharing and reading out loud.

The stories are followed by a variety of creative writing tasks such as writing versions of key events, or describing characters or settings.

The chapters conclude with story-related nonfiction writing tasks, such as writing a postcard, labeling pictures, writing reports, making invitations, and composing a list.

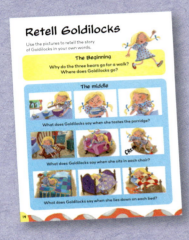

Each activity has an example text, clear instructions, "remember" tips, and useful words to enhance the writing.

Additional activities can be found on pages 30–31.

Encouraging Writing

Using fairy tales as springboards offers children opportunities to have fun writing stories without needing to invent all their own characters or plots. Instead, they could add characters: What if there were seven little pigs instead of three? They could change the setting: What if the bears lived in the city and had made pizza instead of porridge? They could change the ending: What if the glass slipper fitted one of the sisters instead of Cinderella, or if Jack couldn't find the axe? They could imagine what happens "happily ever after" to Jack, the Three Little Pigs, or Cinderella.

The Three Little Pigs

Once upon a time, there were three little pigs. One day, they decided to leave home. "Watch out for the big, bad wolf," said their mother as she waved them goodbye.

The first little pig built a house of straw.

The second little pig built a house of sticks.

The third little pig built a house of bricks.

A big, bad wolf crept up to the house of straw. "Let me in, little pig, let me in," he growled. "Not by the hairs of my chinny chin chin!" said the first little pig.

"Then I'll huff and I'll puff and I'll blow your house in!" cried the big, bad wolf. So, he huffed and he puffed and he blew the house in!

The wolf crept up to the house of sticks.
"Let me in, little pig, let me in," he growled.
"Not by the hairs of my chinny chin chin!" said the second little pig.

"Then I'll huff and I'll puff and I'll blow your house in!" cried the big, bad wolf. So, he huffed and he puffed and he blew the house in.

The wolf crept up to the house of bricks.
"Let me in, little pig, let me in," he growled.
"Not by the hairs of my chinny chin chin!" said the third little pig.

"Then I'll huff and I'll puff and I'll blow your house in!" cried the big, bad wolf. And he huffed and he puffed and he HUFFED and he PUFFED, but he couldn't blow the house of bricks in.

By now the wolf was very angry. He climbed onto the roof.
"I'm coming to get you!" he shouted down the chimney.

The third little pig quickly put a pot of boiling water underneath the chimney. The wolf fell down the chimney straight into the pot! The three little pigs lived happily ever after.

Picture This

These pictures show the main events in **The Three Little Pigs.** Can you remember what they are?

The Beginning

The Middle

The End

Make a Storyboard

This storyboard shows what happened to the pig who built a house of straw.

The first little pig built a house of straw.

A big, bad wolf crept up to the house of straw.

He huffed and he puffed and he blew the house in!

Make your own storyboard for another part of the story.
Draw a picture for each event. Write a caption under each picture.

The Big, Bad Wolf

Draw a picture of the big, bad wolf.
Write some sentences about him under your picture.
Use adjectives to make your sentences interesting.

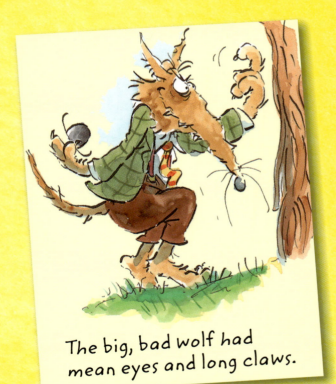

The big, bad wolf had mean eyes and long claws.

Adjectives	Body Parts
black	claws
brown	ears
furry	eyes
long	mouth
mean	nose
pointed	tail
sharp	teeth
stinky	whiskers

★ Remember

• Start sentences with a capital letter and end them with a period.

Sending a Postcard

If the three little pigs sent their mother a postcard, what might they say? The little pig who built his house of bricks might write the message below.

name of the person you are writing to

stamp

Hi Mom,
I've been very busy since I left home. I built myself a house made of bricks. You were right to warn us about the big, bad wolf. He tried to blow my house down, but he couldn't. I hope you are not missing us too much.
Love, Piggy

the message

Mother Pig
3 Pork Place
Swine City, IA
52731

name of the person you are writing to

each part of the address is on a separate line

the name of the sender

Write a Postcard

Write a postcard from a little pig to his mother. You could write a postcard with mother pig's reply.

★ Remember

- Write the message on the left-hand side of the postcard.
- Write the address and draw a stamp on the right-hand side.

A Picture for Your Postcard

On the front of your postcard, draw a picture of one of the little pigs' houses and label it. Add an adjective to each label, such as: blue door.

My House of Bricks

chimney pot

chimney

roof

window

bricks

rain barrel

blue door

Adjectives

blue
brick
large

rectangular
round
shiny

small
tiled
wooden

★ Remember

- Write a heading for your picture.
- Add labels with arrows.

Goldilocks and the Three Bears

Once upon a time, a little girl named Goldilocks went for a walk in the woods. Three bears were also out in the woods. Their porridge was too hot, so they had decided to go for a walk while it cooled down.

Goldilocks found the bears' house in a part of the woods that she had never seen before. By now, she was very hungry and she could smell something delicious coming from inside the house. Goldilocks walked in and saw three bowls of porridge. First, she tried the porridge in the biggest bowl.

"Ouch! Too hot!" she cried. Next, Goldilocks tried the porridge in the medium-sized bowl.

"Yuck! Too cold!" she said. Then she tried the porridge in the smallest bowl.

"Just right!" she said, eating it all up.

After breakfast, Goldilocks wanted to rest. She sat in the biggest chair.

"Ouch! Too hard!" she cried.

Next, she sat in the medium-sized chair.

"Yuck! Too soft!" she cried.

Then she tried the smallest chair. "Just right!" she said. But as she was getting comfortable . . . CRASH! The chair broke into lots of little pieces.

Goldilocks went upstairs and found three beds. She lay down on the biggest bed.

"Ouch! Too hard!" she said. Next, Goldilocks tried the medium-sized bed. It was so soft that it nearly swallowed her up! Then she tried the smallest bed. It felt just right and she fell fast asleep.

Meanwhile, the three bears were finishing their walk.

"Shall we see if our porridge has cooled down?" asked Mama Bear.

"Yes," Baby Bear replied.

"I'm hungry!"

So the three bears hurried back for their breakfast.

"Who's been eating my porridge?" roared Papa Bear.

"Who's been eating my porridge?" asked Mama Bear.

"Who's been eating my porridge?" cried Baby Bear. "They've eaten it all up!"

"Who's been sitting in my chair?" roared Papa Bear.

"Who's been sitting in my chair?" asked Mama Bear.

"Who's been sitting in my chair? They've broken it!" cried Baby Bear.

"Who's been sleeping in my bed?" roared Papa Bear.

"Who's been sleeping in my bed?" asked Mama Bear.

"Look! Someone's still sleeping in my bed!" whispered Baby Bear.

Goldilocks woke up immediately. She jumped out of the window and ran home as fast as she could!

Grrrrrr!

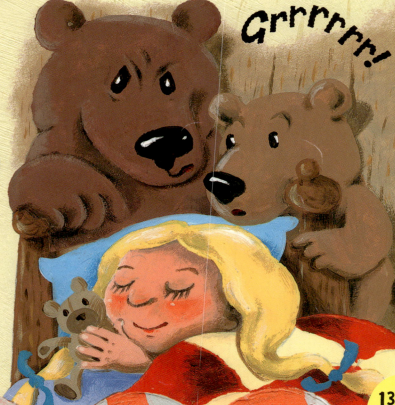

13

Retell Goldilocks

Use the pictures to retell the story of Goldilocks in your own words.

The Beginning

Why do the three bears go for a walk?
Where does Goldilocks go?

The middle

What does Goldilocks say when she tastes the porridge?

What does Goldilocks say when she sits in each chair?

What does Goldilocks say when she lies down on each bed?

What do the three bears say about their bowls of porridge?

What do the three bears say about their chairs?

Grrrrrr!

What do the three bears say about their beds?

The End

What happens at the end?

Here are three ideas for new endings to the story.

1. Goldilocks says sorry and makes the bears some more porridge.
2. Goldilocks makes friends with the three bears and often goes to visit them.
3. The three bears chase Goldilocks all the way to her home and try her breakfast, chair, and bed.

Which ending do you prefer? Why?

Who Are You?

Imagine that the three bears asked Goldilocks some questions like these when she woke up.

Who are you?

Where do you live?

How did you get into our house?

Why did you eat the porridge?

✏️ Ask Questions

Think of some more questions that the three bears might ask Goldilocks.

⭐ Remember

• Use these question words:

Who ...? *What ...?*

Why ...? *When ...?*

How ...? *Where ...?*

• Start your questions with a capital letter and end them with a question mark like this: ?

All About Bears

Here is a report about real brown bears, based on some facts.

Bear Facts

- live in cold mountains and forests
- thick fur keeps them warm
- mostly eat fruit, nuts, roots, and leaves
- dig underground dens for the winter
- sleep in winter for four to six months

Brown Bear Report

Brown bears live in mountains and forests. The weather is cold there, but the bears have thick fur to keep them warm. They eat fruit and nuts. In winter, they dig a den underground. They sleep there until the weather warms up in spring.

Write a Report

Use the facts below about baby bears to write a report.

Baby Bear Facts

- baby bears are called cubs
- born in winter in dens
- usually born in pairs
- drink their mother's milk
- mothers teach cubs how to find food and make dens
- mothers protect cubs from enemies, such as wolves

★ Remember

- Write a title for your report.
- Answer these questions:
  What are baby bears called?
  When are they born?
  Where are they born?
  How many are born?
  What does their mother do?

Cinderella

Once upon a time there was a girl named
Cinderella. She had two stepsisters. One was
tall and one was small. They made Cinderella
work all day long and wear horrible clothing.
They even made her sleep by the fireplace.
Then, one day, a letter arrived.

"It's from the prince!" said the tall stepsister.

"There's a ball at the palace!" said the small stepsister.
Everyone was excited—especially Cinderella. But the stepsisters told her:
"You can't come!"

After the stepsisters left for the ball,
Cinderella sat by the fireplace.

"It's not fair," she said. "I'd love to go
to the ball!"

Suddenly, there was a big flash. It was
a fairy with a wand.

"I'm your fairy godmother," she said.
"Now you can go to the ball!"

The fairy godmother waved her wand. In another flash,
Cinderella had a new dress and sparkling glass slippers.
Then the fairy godmother saw a pumpkin,
four black mice, and a rat. She
waved her wand and, in a flash,
there were four black horses,
a coach, and a coachman.

"Now I can really go to the ball!" said Cinderella.

"Don't forget to be back by twelve!" the fairy godmother shouted.

When Cinderella arrived at the ball, everyone looked at her.

"Who is she?" they all wondered. The stepsisters stared, and the prince couldn't take his eyes off her.

"Will you dance with me?" the prince asked Cinderella. The prince and Cinderella danced and danced and danced all night.

Suddenly, Cinderella heard the clock strike twelve. She ran out of the palace as fast as she could. The prince ran after her, but Cinderella was gone.

"Look! She has left a glass slipper behind!" the prince cried. "Whoever can fit into the slipper will be my princess," he promised.

The prince searched every house in the land. Finally, he arrived at Cinderella's house.

First, the tall sister tried the slipper on. But it was much too small. Then the small stepsister tried it. But it was much too big.

"Now this girl must try it on!" the prince said.

"But that's just Cinderella!" laughed the stepsisters. Cinderella sat down. She tried the glass slipper on. It fitted perfectly.

"Will you be my princess?" asked the prince. Cinderella agreed and they lived happily ever after.

What Happened Next?

This is what happened when the fairy godmother used her magic to help Cinderella.

> The fairy godmother waved her wand. There was a big flash. Cinderella's torn dress turned into a glittering ball gown with stars and flowers. Her worn-out shoes turned into sparkling glass slippers.

Describe the Coach

Write about how the fairy godmother gave Cinderella a coach to ride in. Include some adjectives to make your writing exciting.

Adjectives

black
glossy
golden
grand
magnificent
round
shiny
smart
splendid

pumpkin   rat   mice

coach   coachman

Other Words for Shiny

brilliant
dazzling
gleaming
glittering
sparkling

horses

Perfect Timing

When Cinderella arrived at the ball, this is what happened.

As soon as Cinderella stepped into the ballroom, everyone stopped dancing to stare at her. No one knew who she was. The prince thought Cinderella was the most beautiful girl he had ever seen. He asked her to dance with him. She was thrilled.

Describe the Scene

What happened after the clock struck twelve?

Here are some questions to help you write about it.

1. What did Cinderella do?
2. What happened to her coach, the coachman, and the horses?
3. What did she leave behind?
4. What did the prince do?
5. How did the prince feel?
6. What did he say?

Invitation to the Ball

The prince sent the sisters an invitation to his ball. It told them all about it. Look at how an invitation is written below.

Who is having the party

What kind of party it is

Where the party is

When the party is

What time it starts and ends

What to wear

How to reply

Prince Charming

invites you to his birthday ball at The Grand Palace on Friday, May 15, from 9 P.M. to 12 A.M. Dress: Best clothes

Please let me know if you can come. Telephone 1-800-CHARMING

✏ Write an Invitation

Write your own invitation for a party or a school event, such as a summer fair, a prom, or a book sale. Decorate it to fit the theme of the event.

The Envelope
Put the invitation in an envelope and write the address of the person you are sending it to. Stick on a stamp.

⭐ Remember

- Write each part of the address on a separate line.
- Stick the stamp in the top right-hand corner.

The Sisters
9 Cinder Street
Townsville, CA
95401

Cinderella's List

Cinderella's stepsisters made a long list of all the jobs she had to do for them.

Things to Do

clean the floors
make the beds
wash the clothes
iron the clothes
take out the garbage
do the dishes
prepare supper
serve at the table

Write a List

Write a list of things to do for:
1. looking after a pet
2. cleaning a bike

★ Remember

- Write each thing on your list on a separate line.
- Start each new line with a verb.

Verbs

check	polish
clean	rinse
clear	scrub
empty	sweep
feed	tidy
fix	tighten
fold	wash
grease	wipe

Jack and the Beanstalk

Jack and his mother were very poor. All they had was a cow. One day, Jack went to the market to sell the cow. On the way, Jack met a little old man who wanted to buy the cow.

"I'll give you five magic beans," he told Jack.

When Jack got home, he gave the magic beans to his mother. Jack's mother was very angry. She threw the beans out of the window.

During the night, the magic beans grew and grew. By morning, a beanstalk reached high into the sky. Jack decided to climb the beanstalk. He climbed and climbed and when he reached the top, he found a huge castle! Jack crept inside. Suddenly, the floor began to shake and Jack heard a very loud voice roar:

**"Fee, fi, fo, fum,
I smell the blood of
an Englishman.
Be he alive or be he dead,
I'll grind his bones to
make my bread."**

It was a giant!

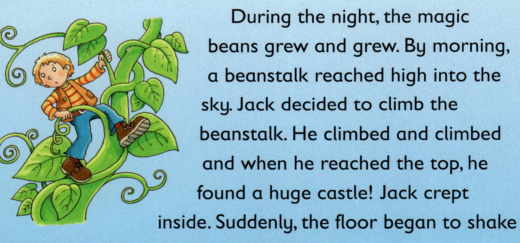

Jack ran into a cupboard to hide. The giant
sat down and ate a huge meal of five sheep.
Then he called for his hen. Jack watched as
the hen laid a perfect golden egg. The giant
was full after his meal and fell asleep. So Jack
crept out of the cupboard and quickly picked
up the giant's hen. But the hen began to
squawk and flap its wings. The giant woke up at once!

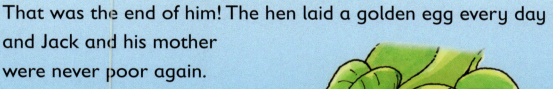

"Fee, fi, fo, fum, I smell the blood of an Englishman!"
he boomed. Jack ran back to the beanstalk and climbed down
as fast as he could.

"I'll get you!" yelled the giant as he chased Jack.

Jack reached the bottom, picked up his ax, and chopped down
the beanstalk. The giant fell to the ground with a thud.
That was the end of him! The hen laid a golden egg every day
and Jack and his mother
were never poor again.

Jack and the Giant

Here is a description of Jack.

Jack was a cheerful boy with red hair, long legs, and a turned-up nose.
He was very thin and often hungry.
His clothes were scruffy and torn.
He was often silly but also very brave.

Describe the Giant

Write a description of the giant.
- How big is he?
- What does he look like?
- What kind of clothes does he wear?
- What kind of person is he?
- How does he move?

Adjectives

angry
bald
cruel
dirty
fierce
grouchy
hairy
mean
mighty
strong
ugly

Other Words for Big

enormous
gigantic
great
huge
immense
massive

⭐ Remember

- Begin each sentence with a capital letter.
- End each sentence with a period.

The Cottage and the Castle

This is a description of the cottage where Jack lives.

Jack's cottage was small. The white walls were covered with ivy and the roof was made of thatch. Its tiny rooms were warm and clean. Jack felt snug and safe here.

Describe the Castle

Write about the giant's castle.

- How big is it?
- What is it built from?
- What is the front door like?
- How many turrets does it have?
- What is it like inside?
- How does it feel inside?
- How many rooms does it have?

Adjectives

cold
damp
creepy
dark
gloomy
gray

large
old
scary
shadowy
stone
vast

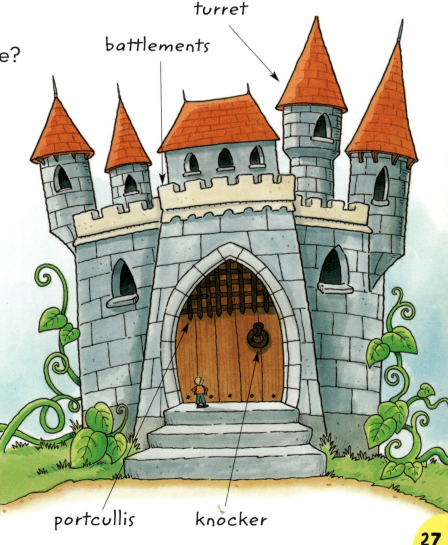

battlements

turret

portcullis   knocker

The Hungry Giant

This is what the giant eats for lunch each day.

On Monday, he crunches crispy chicken.
On Tuesday, he bites boiled bones.
On Wednesday, he chews chunky chops.
On Thursday, he gobbles gristly goat.
On Friday, he feasts on fifty fish.
On Saturday, he swallows salty sheep.
On Sunday, he munches moldy mushrooms.

Dinner Time

Write about what the giant eats for dinner each day. Here are some ideas for meals. Invent your own, too. Use an adjective to describe each dish.

Adjectives

baked
crunchy
fried
juicy
mushy
slimy
stinky
spicy
stale

sausages

chicken

pie

pasta

peas

pizza

jello

fries

Other Words for Eat

devour   munch
feast   nibble
gnaw   nosh
gobble   pig out
guzzle   swallow

★ Remember

- Begin each sentence with a different day of the week.
- Use an adjective for each dish— can you think of one that begins with the same letter as the dish?

28

Jack's Poster

Jack wrote a big poster to tell people about the milk he had for sale.

adjectives that make the milk sound tasty

the list of items for sale

Good Fresh Milk

cup 5¢ glass 10¢
jug 50¢ churn $5
cow $100

the title in large letters to grab people's attention

the price of each item

 **Make a Poster**

Make a poster for a cake or soft drinks stand.

Adjectives

chilled	fresh
chewy	fruity
cool	hot
creamy	iced
crunchy	sweet
delicious	tangy
filling	tasty

 Remember

- Put the name of what you are selling in large letters at the top of the poster.
- Think of some good adjectives to attract attention to your title.
- Make a list of the items for sale.
- Make a list of the price of each item.

More writing ideas

Striking Sentences

Choose a simple sentence from one of the stories, such as
Cinderella ran out of the palace. Think of ways to enrich it.

Vary the verb: Cinderella rushed out of the palace.

Change words: Cinderella dashed down the steps
of the castle.

Add extra words: Upset, Cinderella ran at breakneck
speed out of the magnificent palace.

Add words at the beginning: At the last stroke of the clock,
Cinderella ran out of the palace.

Add words at the end: Cinderella ran out of the palace into the moonlit night.

Add a simile: Quick as a flash, Cinderella ran out of the palace.

Use alliteration: Sad Cinderella skedaddled, sobbing softly.

Choose the Connective

Play this game to help children learn how to vary connectives. Ask them to write
a sentence such as *Jack climbed and climbed ...* and give them a list of connectives,
such as *after, as, as soon as, because, before, but, once, since, until, when, while.*
Ask them to finish the sentence using one of the connectives, eg *Jack climbed and
climbed until he reached the top of the beanstalk.* Or *Jack climbed and climbed
as soon as he had finished breakfast.*

Guess Who?

Ask children to write a description of a fairy-tale character and see if others can
guess who it is, for example, *I am small and pink and have a curly tail.
I built a house of sticks, but a wolf blew it down.*

This edition first published in 2013 by
Sea-to-Sea Publications
Distributed by Black Rabbit Books
P.O. Box 3263, Mankato, Minnesota 56002

Printed in the United States of America,
North Mankato, MN.

9 8 7 6 5 4 3 2

Published by arrangement with the Watts
Publishing Group Ltd, London.

Library of Congress Cataloging-in-Publication Data

Thomson, Ruth, 1949-
 Fairy tales / Ruth Thomson.
    p. cm. -- (It's fun to write)
 ISBN 978-1-59771-406-8 (library binding)
 1. Fairy tales--Authorship--Juvenile literature. I. Title.
 PN3377.5.F32T46 2013
 398.2--dc23

                              2011049892

Series Editor: Melanie Palmer
Series Designer: Peter Scoulding
Consultant: Catherine Glavina, Senior Research Fellow,
Institute of Education, University of Warwick, UK.

Acknowledgments:
The Three Little Pigs: illustrations © Daniel Postgate;
text ©Anne Walter. Goldilocks and the Three Bears:
illustrations ©Anni Axworthy; text © Anne Walter.
Cinderella: illustrations ©Jan McCafferty; text © Anne Cassidy.
Jack and the Beanstalk: illustrations © Steve Cox; text ©Maggie Moore.
Pages 23, 28 (bottom) 29 (middle), illustrations© Franklin Watts.

RD/6000006415/001
May 2012

It's Fun To Write

Fairy Tales

Ruth Thomson

SEA-TO-SEA

Mankato Collingwood London

Grammar Glossary

Nouns

A noun is the name of a person, an animal, an object, or a place.

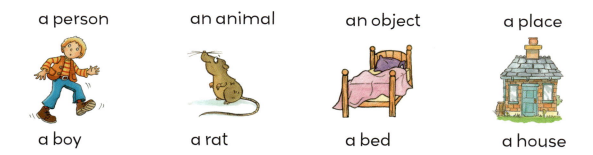

a person	an animal	an object	a place
a boy	a rat	a bed	a house

A proper noun is the name of a particular person or place. A proper noun always begins with a capital letter.

Cinderella   Giant's Castle

Adjectives

An adjective gives more information about a noun. Here are some examples:

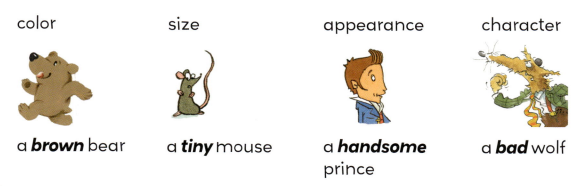

color   size   appearance   character

a **brown** bear   a **tiny** mouse   a **handsome** prince   a **bad** wolf

Verbs

A verb is an action word. It describes what is happening in a sentence.

The pig *built* a house. The wolf *huffed* and *puffed*.

Jack *climbed* up the beanstalk. He *saw* a giant.

Cinderella *danced* all night. She *heard* the clock strike.

Below are some additional writing activities related to each story.

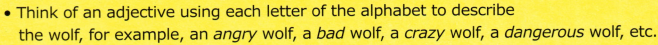

The Three Little Pigs
- Think of an adjective using each letter of the alphabet to describe the wolf, for example, an *angry* wolf, a *bad* wolf, a *crazy* wolf, a *dangerous* wolf, etc.
- Think of silly alternatives to the wolf's refrain, such as *"I'll huff and I'll puff and I'll ... clean your windows."*
- Make some "No entrance" and other signs to keep out the wolf.
- Write a list of materials the third little pig used to build his house.
- Retell *The Three Little Pigs* in a folding book, using days of the weeks as the structure, for example, **On Monday**, *the little pigs left home.*

    On Tuesday, *one little pig built a house of straw,* etc.

Goldilocks and the Three Bears
- Pretend you are a police officer investigating the break-in at the bears' house. Think of questions to ask the bears. Remember to use the question words: *Who? Where? When? What? Why? How?*
- Write a letter of apology from Goldilocks to Baby Bear and his reply.
- Reverse the roles and imagine what the three bears do in Goldilocks' house and what she and her family might say.

Cinderella
- Write a few sentences of Cinderella's diary for the week leading up to, and including, the ball. Start each entry with a different day of the week, for example, **On Monday**, *I mended and washed the sisters' ball gowns.*
- Imagine a conversation between the two sisters after the ball. Use other words for *said*, to show how the sisters felt, such as *bellowed, shrieked, screamed, squeaked, declared, hissed, howled, grumbled, sniveled, sobbed, gasped*, etc.

Jack and the Beanstalk
- Make a list of other words ending in *-um* (using a rhyming dictionary might be helpful) and make up alternative rhymes for the giant's refrain, such as *Fee, fo, fi, fum, I hear the beat of a soldier's drum.*
- Imagine what would have happened if Jack had traded the cow for some rutabaga seeds instead and had an adventure underground.
- Find out how beans grow and write a report about them.
- Tell the story from the giant's point of view. Call it **The Giant and the Beanstalk.** Think about how he feels when Jack breaks into his home and steals his hen.